Old KINROSS-SHIRE

by

Guthrie Hutton and David Millar

Kinross Junction Station has been so completely erased from the landscape by the M90 motorway that the only things to survive are a street name, fading memories and old pictures. This one gives a good impression of how busy and important the station was, but alas, does not show the flowers and model of Loch Leven Castle that used to adorn the platform and make it a pleasant place for passengers to await the arrival of their train.

ACKNOWLEDGEMENTS

The authors would like to thank all those people who offered
anecdotes and information to enrich the stories in this book.
We also wish to thank Barbara McCutcheon and Bill Fiet who
helped by supplying pictures.

SOME FURTHER READING

These books used during the authors' research are not
available from Stenlake Publishing. Anyone interested in
finding out more is advised to contact their local bookshop
or library.

Beath, David, *The Bishopshire and its People*, 1902.
Bruce, William Scott, *The Railways of Fife*, 1980.
Copeland, John, *Roads and Their Traffic 1750–1850*, 1968.
Day, J. P., *The Counties of Clackmannan and Kinross*, 1915.
Duncan, Jeremy, *Perth and Kinross, the Big County*, 1997.
Fossoway and District Community Council, *The Annals of
    Kinross-shire*, 1990.
Haynes, Nick, *Perth and Kinross, An Illustrated Architectural
    Guide*, 2000.
Kinross Antiquarian Society, *Historical Guide to the County
    of Kinross*, 1980.
Munro, David M., *Kinross in Old Picture Postcards*, 1985.
Smith, David J., *Action Stations*, second edition 1989.
T.M.T., *Glimpses of Kinross-shire in the Past*, 1935.
Watson, John. F., *Views of Kinross-shire*, a calendar from
    1988.
Vernon, Edward, *The Complete Works of Michael Bruce*, 1951.
Young, Robert S., *About Kinross-shire and Its Folk*, 1948.

Also by Guthrie Hutton for Stenlake Publishing:
Old Alloa ISBN 1 84033 223 9
Old Clackmannan, Sauchie, Tullibody and other airts of the Wee County ISBN 1 84033 238 7
Old Hillfoots ISBN 1 84033 242 5
Old Perth ISBN 1 872074 48 0

For details of prices and availability of these books, please visit www.stenlake.co.uk or
phone 01290 551122. All orders to UK addresses are post-free.

Scouting was started in Kinross-shire in 1910 followed a few years later by Guiding,
although this picture at Milnathort's 'big' primary school is thought to have been taken
in the 1940s. The set faces and black armband suggest that these leaders have gathered
for a melancholy occasion like a funeral or memorial service. From the left they are:
Scout District Commissioner and Group Scout Leader (Milnathort), Tom Graham;
Guide County Commissioner Clementine Montgomery and Scout Area Commissioner,
Walter Scott-Davidson. As with civic affairs in the county, the Scout movement has
seen its original area and district local structure superseded by a larger, single-tier, area
administration for the whole of Perth & Kinross.

INTRODUCTION

'Old Kinross' was typical of the random jumble of houses, stairs and streets that once made up the centre of Scottish towns. The parts that remain are delightful, but this corner appears to have succumbed to the march of time.

Kinross-shire had the second smallest area and the smallest population of any county in Scotland when it was linked with Perthshire in 1930 to bring core functions like policing, fire services and education under the larger authority and thus ease the financial burden on Kinross. This connection was strengthened in the local government reorganisation of 1974 which created a two tier system of regional and district authorities. When the upper, regional, tier was scrapped in 1996 the district authority became Perth & Kinross Council, thus cementing the link with Perth. This union, however, is not the only one Kinross has had with its neighbours and in some ways is not the most obvious. It shares a parliamentary constituency with Clackmannanshire and a postcode with Fife. Before the advent of a national water authority its water supplies were run in conjunction with authorities in Fife and even the local newspaper was taken over in 1970 by a Fife-based publisher.

Fife certainly had strong historical links with Kinross and at one time the two formed part of a larger area known as Fife and Fothriff, but while Fife survived the lottery of history, Fothriff did not. It appears to have broken up into smaller areas and of these the parishes of Kinross, Orwell and part of Portmoak were formed into the nucleus of a county in 1426. This was enlarged in 1685 with the addition of the remaining part of Portmoak, Cleish and Tullibole parishes and the Barony of Cuthilgourdy from southern Perthshire.

Kinross-shire is like a saucer surrounded by a rim of hills. This is formed in the north and west by the Ochils and in the west and south by the Cleish Hills. Benarty occupies the south-east corner while the Lomond Hills guard the east. Gaps between these hills almost invited railways and roads to march through, placing Kinross historically at the heart of Scotland. The county has no connection to the sea, but it does include Loch Leven, the largest body of water in lowland Scotland and one that has made a big contribution to the county's story.

Agriculture has long been a mainstay of the county, but secondary industry has largely passed it by. Coal was mined in the south and for a time the town of Kinross was noted for making cutlery, but ultimately it could not compete with Sheffield's huge industry. The town also boasted a linen industry, but this too came to an end when faced with competition from Dunfermline's linen weavers. Hand-loom weaving was carried on in hundreds of cottages throughout the county making cloth for the large Glasgow and Dunfermline manufacturers, and this tradition in textiles continues today with the cashmere mill that is the county's main industrial employer.

This slight industrial activity has long been a concern, but despite the anxieties over this and the county's contradictory links with its neighbours, Kinross-shire has sailed into the twenty-first century with its sense of identity intact. Kinross Community Council produces a popular newsletter, while pop festivals and markets shout the name to the nation's rooftops, and – whisper it softly – there is even a 'Free Kinross-shire' movement. This is one place and space that should be watched!

Sitting on its small island out in the loch, Loch Leven Castle was clearly once a place of some strength. The earliest masonry suggests structural work beginning in the late thirteenth or early fourteenth century, with the main tower house dating from the 1320s. It was a royal castle which King Robert II granted to Sir Henry Douglas in 1390, and although his family held it for nearly 300 years it continued to be used for state purposes during this time, notably as a prison. The most famous prisoner was of course Mary Queen of Scots whose enemies brought her to the castle after the battle of Carberry Hill in June 1567. While there she was forced to abdicate in favour of her infant son who became James VI

and also, in 1603, James I of England. Helped by the keeper of the castle's boats Mary escaped in May 1568, but within days her forces were defeated at the battle of Langside. She fled to England, only to endure another nineteen years of captivity before being executed. The Douglas connection with Loch Leven Castle ceased in 1672 when it was sold to the Surveyor of the King's Works in Scotland, Sir William Bruce. He appears to have lived in it while his own grand house on the shores of the loch was being built. The castle does not appear to have been occupied after he left it, but the great tower house and perimeter wall survived in good order, as these wintry scenes from the early twentieth century show.

Sir William Bruce was the son of a Fife laird who supported the royalist cause before the Restoration and later rose to high office in the service of King Charles II. He is not thought to have been formally trained as an architect, but to have acquired knowledge of design and construction during travels to Europe and England, and experience by carrying out modifications to existing buildings. His foremost patron, the 2nd Earl (later Duke) of Lauderdale, was a trusted favourite of the king and perhaps the most powerful man in Scotland. Bruce no doubt owed his position to his influential patron and, in his role as Surveyor of the King's Works, had the task of remodelling Holyrood Palace. This was completed in 1678 and, relieved of his official position, he spent the remaining years of his life as an architect. His principal project was to design and build his own mansion, Kinross House, which was positioned with gardens framing a vista of Loch Leven Castle. The building, constructed under the direction of master mason Tobias Bauchop of Alloa, was begun c.1686 and took about five years to complete. It is one of the great milestones of Scottish architectural history, linking the vernacular architecture of the mid-seventeenth century with the more sophisticated Adam period.

Kinross, the old county capital, straddled the Great North Road at a point approximately midway between Queensferry and Perth. This location gave the town a strategic significance in the days when travelling meant a not very fast coach ride. Kinross became an overnight stop with, for a town of its size, a larger than average number of inns catering for the weary travellers. This view along High Street was the first that travellers from the south would have had of the town, although the railway had superseded coaches by the time most of the buildings here were built. The coach travellers would of course recognise the parish church steeple, which was built about 1761, some twenty years after the church itself. A special committee was formed to raise funds to build the steeple, but instead of disbanding when that was done it remained in existence as an early town council. The church was demolished in 1832, but the steeple was left standing as a landmark in the town centre; its clock was replaced in 1875. The town hall was erected on the site of the old church in 1841, but time appears to have caught up with it too and another cycle of change seems likely around the base of the old steeple.

Kinross High Street on a day when a bicycle, two cars and a wee van from Fife were the only vehicles in town; and this before the traffic was diverted away from the town centre by the motorway. The distinctive-looking building behind the van was the old tolbooth, the one-time civic centre, courthouse and jail. Dating from the early seventeenth century, it was remodelled in 1771 by the great Scottish architect and local landowner, Robert Adam, with the unusual bowed frontage forming part of his work. A prominent plaque on the second floor proclaims that Adam, who was MP for Kinross-shire at the time, 'decorated this front at his own expense' – a gesture which no doubt helped to promote his image, and one which today's politicians, reliant on a fickle and transient media to provide their 'spin', must envy! On the left-hand edge of the picture is the Cross Well Fountain dating from 1893, a time when civic fountains were springing up(!) all over the country. The well had previously been used as the town's public water supply.

The kirk steeple dominates this view looking south down the High Street. Immediately in front of the steeple is a small, early nineteenth century tenement block – 98–102 High Street – which is interesting because it was built with an angled frontage to follow the street line. On the other side of the street, the two adjacent buildings with their gables facing the road have gone, a loss which has robbed the present day view of some interest. In the left foreground is one of the town's old coaching inns, the Salutation Hotel. The hotel's original entrance from the High Street has a fine lintel stone dated 1721, but the doorway it used to span is now a window. Many other alterations and extensions have been made to the structure over the years leaving a fascinating exterior that almost demands to be read and interpreted by students of architecture. Perhaps those who come to drool over Kinross House should be made to examine the Salutation Hotel as well – before they visit the bar!

HIGH STREET, KINROSS. *Looking North.*

On the left of this early twentieth century picture looking north along High Street is Sands' ironmongery, which still operates as a hardware store under the name of John & J. H. Sands – a remarkable survival in this world of constant change. The shop was founded by a Joseph Hardie who passed it on to his nephew, David Sands, in 1846. He was already trading as a general merchant selling cheese, tea, stationery, glue, gunpowder and other products and by the 1860s was also offering taxidermy, no doubt stuffing all those prize trout that were fished out of the loch. David Sands' three sons – John, Joseph Hardie and David – took over in 1881, but within a few years brotherly tensions had caused a split. David set up his own grocery business while the others carried on trading as general merchants and ironmongers under the company name of John & J. H. Sands. The Sands connection ended in 1973 when the last family member in the business retired, but the new owners retained the name following a management buy-out. The separate grocery business established by David Sands, however, still remains in the family and operates a string of local supermarkets, one of which has taken over the whole corner site from the hardware store into Station Road.

Dates on the facades of villas in this early twentieth century view of Station Road range from 1889 to 1904, indicating that this west end of the road was not developed for residential use until the railway was completed from Edinburgh to Perth. As well as going to the station, the road had always been the principal thoroughfare to the west of Kinross and has undergone some changes since this picture was taken. Housing, set back from the road, has been built on the field to the left and the primary school and Kinross Tennis Club now occupy the ground to the right. The wall on the right has also been removed allowing the road to be widened and a footpath made on each side, while the volume of traffic today would make it inadvisable to walk down the middle of the carriageway with a pram. The square tower in the distance is that of the Parish Church. It was built to an 'off the shelf' design which the architect George Angus had already used at Kincardine and Kingskettle in Fife and was opened for divine service in March 1832. The church sits at the gushet formed by Station Road and Swansacre where a drinking fountain acts as a memorial to James Mungle, a physician who practised in the town for 21 years.

High Street, Kinross has a more spacious appearance to the north of the town centre, as this view from around 1900 shows. It favours the sunny, east side of the street where the County Buildings can be seen on the extreme left. These were erected about 1826/27, superseding those remodelled by Robert Adam in the centre of the town. The railings at the front have gone, presumably to provide iron to make munitions during World War II, and the war memorial now stands in front of the building. The Clydesdale Bank occupies a villa of 1820s date where the clump of trees just right of centre can be seen. On the other side of the street are the Burgh Chambers and another former coaching inn, the Kirklands Hotel. In their day, these inns also provided a place to keep the coaches and stabling for the horses, and when motor vehicles appeared on the roads this was often converted into garaging for cars belonging to hotel residents. This process was taken a step further by the Kirklands Garage, adjacent to the hotel, where the villa that once nestled behind the hedge on the right became the site of a garage and filling station which now looks very old-fashioned in these days of multi-pump, self-service forecourts.

The early nineteenth century expansion of Kinross to the north also included the school, built in 1823 opposite the site where the County Buildings were erected three years later. The original school was progressively extended and is now Kinross High School, but to make room for this expansion the old school eventually had to be demolished. Its bell forms part of a memorial erected in stone by pupils of the school's technical department in 1969. These boys, with their drawing boards, sample display and a wooden plant stand appear to be from an earlier technical class. The picture was used as a postcard in 1914.

Of all the factors affecting the development of Kinross over the centuries, the coming of the motorway and the huge expansion of car use have made the most significant impact. They have encouraged the rapid development of housing schemes and these now present the dominant image of Kinross. It's as if the town went into expansion overdrive, but in a sense this simply accelerated the development that had begun before the motorway was built. Through the first half of the twentieth century the town grew steadily out towards the Muirs of Kinross, the moorland that gave this road, the Muirs, its name. Some of the earlier housing developments are seen here in this view looking south along the Muirs with Gallowhill Road leading off to the right. The building on the corner, with its little turret roof, was formerly The Corner Shop. In its heyday it was adorned with advertising for all the major chocolate and cocoa makers – Cadbury's, Fry's and Rowntree's – but now some of these 'household names' no longer exist and the shop is a house.

Gallowhill Road heads out of town to this group of corrugated-iron buildings opposite the entrance to Gallowhill Farm. They were built in the early twentieth century as a fever hospital. In those days, before the discovery of antibiotics, the only way medical science could combat contagious infection like phthisis (pulmonary tuberculosis) was to place sufferers in isolation. This policy extended to the hospital having its own horse-drawn ambulance to bring the patients in, and once admitted they could be quarantined, without visitors, for up to six weeks. The timber-framed, corrugated-iron construction of these buildings was quick to erect and often used in the early twentieth century for sanatoria and fever hospitals. Few survive, but this group became a youth hostel when its medical days were over and is now in private ownership. The farm name is no doubt taken from a gallows that stood at nearby Lathro from the late fifteenth century until the Heritable Jurisdiction Act of 1748 abolished them.

We've all done it, taken a picture and almost missed the subject, as has happened with this shot of Balado Station – although almost missing a railway station is quite a miss! The station, originally known as Cleish Road, was on the Devon Valley Railway which ran from Alloa to Kinross Junction by way of Dollar. Balado, however, is perhaps best known for another form of transport – flying. The airfield – known as Balado Bridge – was opened in March 1942 during the Second World War. It operated in conjunction with Grangemouth airfield, being used for the advanced training of pilots who had undergone initial instruction at the parent field. After the war, McDonnell Aircraft of Milnathort (not to be confused with the McDonnell Aircraft Corporation [now part of Boeing] of St Louis, Missouri) broke up hundreds of redundant aircraft at the airfield. During that time it continued to be used by light aircraft and gliders which were launched by a winch, or by being towed by a car or small aeroplane. The gliding activity that started at Balado is now carried on at the Scottish Gliding Centre at Portmoak. The airfield closed in 1957, but Balado's associations with flying objects remained; in the 1980s a NATO ground satellite station, with a highly conspicuous 'giant golf ball', was set up. The site is now also famous as the venue for the 'T in the Park' pop music festival, which fairly wakes the echoes in Kinross and the surrounding area. The thousands of people who come to hear the music might find it easier to get to the site if the railway had not been closed in 1964.

As railways spread across the country, the first tracks to advance into Kinross-shire came from the east. The Fife & Kinross Railway, which ran through Stratheden from Ladybank, was opened to Milnathort in March 1858 and to Kinross by the following August. Another line, the Kinross-shire Railway, headed north from near Cowdenbeath and was connected to the F&K in 1860. These lines, which became part of the giant North British Railway in the 1860s, formed a continuous loop through Kinross-shire from one part of Fife to the other. This situation prevailed until 1890, when following completion of the Forth Bridge, the NBR extended the line from Mawcarse through Glenfarg to Bridge of Earn, putting the Kinross-shire stations on a through route between Edinburgh and Perth. Services on this skilfully engineered and valuable route ceased in 1970, but the stations at Mawcarse and here at Milnathort were earlier casualties of railway cutbacks, closing in June 1964.

Milnathort's origins as a market town are thought to go back to an annual tryst on Cuthill Muir where thousands of lambs were bought and sold. Other sales were held at different times and places throughout the county until a William Bethune held the first recognisable auction mart in the 1860s. This was a time when more organised and frequent sales were becoming established around the country, one of which was run at Dollar by a George Young. In 1874 he extended his activities east, to Milnathort, setting up a permanent mart adjacent to the railway in 1877, and later amalgamating with William Bethune to form Young, Bethune & Co. They faced competition from a number of other auctioneers – Robert Young; Oliver & Sons of Edinburgh; and Hay & Co. of Perth – and later merged with another Perth auctioneer, Macdonald Fraser & Co. Over time the larger markets at Perth and elsewhere grew at the expense of the smaller country sales and Milnathort's mart eventually sold its last animal. The site is now known as the Auld Mart Business Park and this, along with Auld Mart Road and Auld Mart Lane, has perpetuated the name.

Pedestrians and cyclists appear to have banished all other transport from South Street in this view looking south from the cross. South Street was Milnathort's main shopping thoroughfare and around 1930, when this picture was used as a postcard, the shop on the extreme left was a drapery owned by Balneaves. They employed a number of dressmakers and tailors, and the clothes they made were worn by many people from Milnathort and the surrounding area. Once people had kitted themselves out at Balneaves, they could have their boots and shoes repaired next door, and buy a camera to record the sartorial results at the camera and stationery shop next to that. This was run by Andrew Gardiner, who published his own photographs as postcards and sold them at the shop. They provide a splendid record of the county, principally in the Milnathort area, and many of them appear in this book. More recently, ironmonger Arnold Henderson occupied Balneaves' shop, Colin Brough was still running the cobbler's business, Andrew Gardiner's shop was a newsagency run by George Temple and next to that was George Hart's draper's business.

The Great North Road that brought large volumes of coaching traffic to the Kinross hotels also delivered patrons to Milnathort's hotels. These were mainly grouped around the cross which was formed by the meeting of this road – formerly the A90 – Wester Loan and the A91 road along the Ochil Hillfoots from Stirling to St Andrews. An old road sign can be seen poking out from behind the building on the left. It shows the A90 and A91 as a combined route going east from the cross; they went their separate ways again a mile further east, at Arlary. The A90 has of course been superseded through the county by the M90 which has consigned the once mighty Great North Road to B class ignominy as the B996. Queen Victoria passed along the road in 1842 on her way to Balmoral and 10,000 spectators are reported to have lined the route through Kinross and Milnathort. The occasion apparently prompted the proprietor of the hotel on the left-hand edge of the picture to change its name to the Royal – its former name is thought to have been the Swan. The queen passed through the county again in 1879 when her train slowed outside Milnathort to let her look at Loch Leven. The Royal Hotel was sold in 1866 to a new owner from Cupar who paid the princely sum of £605 for it. It has had a number of other owners since then, as has the Commercial Hotel, in the background, which is now the Jolly Beggars.

Milnathort's cross is distinguished by the town hall and its 95-foot high clock steeple. It was built with funds raised by public subscription and opened in 1855. As well as a hall, the building also provided accommodation for the local police constable and cells for his customers. The white house in front is older than the steeple – a fact that even the most amateur of historical sleuths can deduce, because the door lintel is dated 1792. The house was the residence of the miller who operated the meal mill, the large building on the right-hand edge of the picture.

The mill would have been the principal supplier of oatmeal and flour for the area, but was put out of action in 1861 and again in 1912 by fires; the latter spectacular blaze is seen here. Mill fires were common because the dust created by the milling process can have the same explosive combustibility as coal dust. The mill was latterly operated by the firm of Gray & Harrower, but when they moved to new premises on the Stirling Road the building fell into disrepair. It has since been demolished and flats have been built on the site.

MILNATHORT, MILL on FIRE MARCH 5TH 1912.

The Orwell Parish Church is prominent in the background of this view looking north from the tower of the town hall. This austere little church was erected here in 1729 using stones from the old church near Loch Leven, and was remodelled in the 1880s. There is some modern housing close to the church and the motorway runs behind it, discreetly hidden in a deep cutting. In the middle distance, to the left, some children are playing in the grounds of the primary school which was situated in Manse Road. The school can be seen behind the open-fronted shed which was used by the children to shelter when playtime coincided with bad weather. Primary education in Milnathort was carried out in two buildings; this one was used for the older children and known as the 'big' school while the 'wee' school, for infants, was in Stirling Road. In the years following World War II the children from both schools came together in the town hall to eat school dinners provided by the education authority.

The 'wee' school for Milnathort's younger primary school children was the Reid Memorial School, the church-like building in the centre of this view of Stirling Road. It was named after Mrs Reid of Thomanean who gifted it to the education authority in 1895. The school was superseded in the 1970s and demolished, but the bell was saved and set up as a small memorial on the former site in a stone-built surround, not unlike that at Kinross High School. The site where the school stood is now a car park, and if anyone using it needs someone to look at their vehicle, Stewart & Smart's modern filling station, garage and showroom now occupy the adjacent area and continue the work of the old garage seen on the right. Opposite the garage, just poking into the left-hand edge of the picture, is a building known as the Salt House. Salt was a valuable commodity in the days before fridges and freezers because people could use it to preserve various foodstuffs.

The tale of Milnathort's two primary schools continues with this Andrew Gardiner picture of Stirling Road, looking east into the village. The 'wee' Reid Memorial School and the 'big' school in Manse Road were both superseded in the 1970s by a new Milnathort Primary School, which was erected on the site seen here on the right. Just beyond the gas street lamp is the gushet with Church Street (known as Inchmerrie before acquiring its present name). The street's closeness to Stirling Road and its similar line suggests that it was an early route into old Milnathort which was superseded by the later Stirling Road. The spire of the United Free Church, on the corner of South Street and Church Street, is prominent in the distance. It was built in the 1860s to the designs of a Kilmarnock architect but has now been converted into housing. A little to the west, on the other side of Church Street, is the old United Presbyterian Church building now used by South Lissens Pottery. The church was formed about 1761 and this austere, four-square building suggests that its congregation practised a strict form of worship.

Back Loan and Old Perth Road originally formed the main route to the north through Milnathort. It was a typically narrow old Scots village thoroughfare with a ford at the cross where the Back Burn ran over it. In Back Loan, where some door lintels bear dates from the late seventeenth century, buildings encroached unevenly from either side, a situation guaranteed to delay traffic. As this was one of the country's busiest and most important thoroughfares it was replaced by a new road – called New Road. A date stone of 1790 on the Back Burn bridge suggests that this is when it was created, and another of 1939 on the back of the bridge parapet suggests that this is when the roads at the cross were raised. New Road formed a through route with Stirling Road which carried increasing volumes of traffic as motor vehicles took over from horses. There was clearly fierce competition for the passing trade, as this picture shows. A couple of petrol pumps can be seen outside the Thistle Hotel, to the left of the many pumps outside W. Keir & Son's garage. The photographer, possibly Andrew Gardiner, has used the gas street lamp to good effect in this picture and in the one on the previous page, but photography was deprived of these valuable foreground features when they were replaced by electric lighting in 1945.

The cart heading east along New Road here looks like a 'soor dook cairt' – one that sold buttermilk. It is passing the Thistle Hotel, a hostelry that adapted to changing times over the years. The area in front of the main hotel building has now been enclosed to form a lounge bar and restaurant, but in the picture on the facing page it is taken up with petrol pumps, and here it is simply an open space for passengers to get on and off carriages. The Thistle was an inn in the days of stagecoach travel, and when that ceased it continued to cater for horse-hauled traffic. The sign on the building jutting out towards the road indicates that it was a posting establishment – a place which hired out riding horses and horses to pull private carriages. It would also have hired post-chaises – carriages with a driver known as a post-boy who, despite the name, could be a crusty old veteran. The arched doorway is now a window, but formerly led to the carriage yard and stables which could apparently hold up to 40 horses.

With no coastline, Kinross-shire could never aspire to having any sort of a links, so despite being on the road to the home of golf at St Andrews the game does not appear to have taken hold in the county until the late nineteenth century. It then made up for lost time, because in a comparatively short time four courses were established, including this one at Milnathort. Its club was formed in 1910 to play on a nine-hole course laid out on parkland to the south-east of the village, and its continuing use since then has required the old clubhouse, seen here, to be upgraded and modernised. There was a small course adjacent to Kinross Station at one time, although when Kinross Golf Club was formed in 1884 it played on a course which was laid out by Tom Morris, one of the leading men in his field at the time, and went 'from the Kirkgate to the Factor's Pier'. This now forms part of two very fine eighteen-hole courses operated by the largest of the old Kinross coaching inns, the Green Hotel. These occupy a large swathe of land between the town and Loch Leven and offer players a variety of golfing challenges while they enjoy fine views across the loch. Views over the loch are also a feature of the nine-hole Bishopshire course on the lower slopes of Bishop Hill at Kinnesswood. It was opened in 1913, replacing an earlier course.

The picture below from about 1918 shows Mayfield Cottage on Burleigh Road. This once isolated location at the edge of the village was later overtaken by housing developments on the field in front and the area to the left. Now, more modern houses have pushed the village even further out along the road towards Burleigh Castle. The road jouks around its gatehouse, making the castle one of the most visible in the country. Burleigh came into the possession of the Balfour family in 1446 and the sturdy-looking keep appears to date from their occupancy in the second half of the fifteenth century. The only remaining section of courtyard wall, with an

Burleigh Castle, Milnathort.

arched gateway in it, connects the keep to a gate tower dating from 1582. This is corbelled out to a squared top from a rounded base pierced by shot holes; defensive measures that were probably augmented by a moat surrounding the whole structure. These were most likely intended only for security and not because the occupants were engaged in overt hostilities. The Balfour family supported the Stuart royal family and held positions at court, but this led to support for the Jacobite cause in 1715 which in turn resulted in forfeiture of Burleigh Castle and its ultimate descent into ruin.

Coastal shipping moved much of the country's trade and commerce in the days before railways, but a wholly inland county like Kinross-shire was reliant on the roads. This was not a good position to be in, because Scotland's roads had never been good and in many cases were little more than tracks used by trains of pack-horses. However, as industry and commerce began to grow through the latter end of the eighteenth century things began to get better. Roads were improved and in some cases completely replaced, but although the work was authorised by government it was carried out by road trustees who recovered the money they spent by charging tolls. Toll gates and toll houses had been around for some time, but this period of expansion saw many more being erected. They were not popular and the system ended in the 1870s, leaving a legacy of toll houses around the country. One of the most impressive is this one at Balgedie which claims a sixteenth century origin. It used to control two roads, so would have been doubly disliked, but in losing its original function it has found a new popularity – as a pub.

This church, with its manse in the foreground, stood on the southern edge of Easter Balgedie. It was used by a congregation that was part of a movement which seceded from the Church of Scotland and sowed seeds of dissent that simmered for over a century. At issue was who should have the right to appoint a minister; the congregation, or a powerful patron. The argument burst into the open in 1843 when dissidents left the established church in droves to form the Church of Scotland Free, or Free Church. The period is known in church history as the Disruption, but it was not the first time that congregations had formed new churches, and Kinross-shire was at the forefront of the dissension. A monument at Gairney Bridge marks the occasion in 1733 when the first breakaway took place, and although divisions amongst the seceders resulted in a number of small churches being formed, the movement was very strong in the county. Balgedie's United Presbyterian Church played its part. It was set up about 1800 and its minister, the Revd William Mackelvie, was chosen as Moderator for the United Presbyterian Synod in 1856. Prior to that, in 1837, he had published a small volume of poems by the notable local poet Michael Bruce, who was also an adherent to the secession church.

Michael Bruce, the 'Gentle Poet of Loch Leven', was born the son of a weaver in Kinnesswood on 27 March 1746. He started his education at the village school and from there went to Edinburgh University. On completing his studies he returned to Kinross-shire and became a teacher at Gairney Bridge, but he left after a short time to study at the 'theological hall' of the secession church in Kinross. He took up another teaching post at Forestmill in Clackmannanshire, but while there contracted tuberculosis and returned home to Kinnesswood. He died at the age of 21 on 6 July 1767. In his short life he gained a reputation as a scholar and poet, writing a number of verses and some religious paraphrases. The cottage where he grew up was purchased in 1868 by two local antiquaries from Kinross, David Marshall and Robert Burns-Begg, a grand nephew of that other poet, Robert Burns. Their intention was to form an association to collect items relevant to the poet's life and work, and open the cottage as a memorial. They managed to keep the building in good order and, after both had died, a trust was formed in 1903 to continue their efforts. The cottage, in the village street called The Cobbles, was opened as a museum in 1906.

The area to the east of Loch Leven was once part of the Bishopric of St Andrews and this connection has conferred on it the 'county within a county' name of the Bishopshire. Kinnesswood, nestling at the foot of Bishop Hill, is the largest of the area's villages, although for a while it seems to have existed in a state of suspension, untroubled by the march of time. On seeing this state of completeness, mischievous visitors were known to observe that it was nice to see that the building of the village was 'finished'; but changes have taken place over time. Modern housing has extended the village in almost every direction and has spread into the old streets too. This group of houses, just up from Michael Bruce's cottage, occupied a patch of ground between The Cobbles and Back Dykes Road. They are hard to recognise now and the old name, Wallace Square, seems to have disappeared. The building lines remain, although upgrading and reconstruction have changed the appearance of most houses and left the dyke and kerbed walkway in the left foreground as the most obvious link to the past.

The post office and village shop in the right foreground of this picture looking north has long been the focal point of life in Kinnesswood. It was run by the Sharp family for many years, and they did not confine their business activities to the shop's four walls. David Sharp also owned a horse and gig with which he met trains at Mawcarse Junction Station, taking passengers on to destinations throughout the Bishopshire and beyond. The horse-drawn taxi became a motorised one after Tom Buchan, a former mine-worker from Kelty, married into the family. He set up the garage across the road from the post office and with a seven seater Austin carried anyone – from tattie howkers to wedding parties – around the area. The garage still exists, although it sells a different brand of petrol to the once popular Pratt's on offer here, and Kinross County Council no longer exists to issue the registration letters SV which the wee van has on its number plate. The public telephone advertised by the post office was long ago superseded by a phone box outside, although in these days of almost universal mobile phone use, it too is becoming a quaint thing of the past.

The Bishopshire's religious associations are said to have been the stimulus for the industry that Kinnesswood was famous for; the manufacture of vellum and parchment. It is thought to have begun with the monks on St Serf's Island in Loch Leven either making it or simply stimulating the industry by being its best customers. Either way, few other places made these materials and so Scotland's archives probably contain many documents written on Kinnesswood products. This industry is unlikely to have created much wealth for local people, but it was a more certain way to make money than the one that burst upon the Bishopshire in 1852. Word got out that there was gold in 'them thar' Lomond Hills and within three weeks thousands of people were swarming over the area in search of riches. They also discovered that they had to search for food, because with so many prospectors in such small villages the local shops were quickly cleaned out. The shopkeepers were the only ones to make a killing because the 'gold' turned out to be a valueless mineral, galena, or fool's gold!

South of Kinnesswood is the village of Scotlandwell, known in ancient times as Fons Scotiae. The Bishop of St Andrews established a thirteenth century ministry here dedicated to the Virgin Mary, and the 'Red Friars of Scotlandwell' are said to have set up a hospice for people who came to drink from the well of spring water. It became famed in the thirteenth century for its powers to heal ailments such as leprosy, a disease which afflicted King Robert the Bruce who is known to have visited the well in 1329 in the hope of a cure. Water still flows from the well which is protected by a roof structure, like a lych-gate, which was erected by the local laird, Sir Charles Bruce of nearby Arnot Tower. The well is located off to the left of this picture, down a short road hidden by the building on the left which was the Portmoak School. The view looks north along the main street of the village with the road to Leslie leading off on the right in front of the cottage behind the white horse. This cottage, which is thought to have been a toll house, had been demolished before the first decade of the twentieth century had ended.

By 1777 Portmoak School, the parochial school at Kinnesswood where Michael Bruce received his early education, was regarded as being too small and inconvenient and so a new school was built at Scotlandwell. That building was superseded in 1834 by the one in the picture on the facing page, and further change will have followed the mandatory provisions of the Education Act of 1872. The school has since moved back to Kinnesswood, and because the date of this picture of a junior class is not known the location is likewise uncertain. It could be either Scotlandwell or Kinnesswood, but whichever one it was the girl who used the photograph as a Christmas card seemed happy enough. She was from near Glenfarg and wrote that she did 'have not far to go to school', which, if a touch ungrammatical, is an interesting comment on the way people's perception of time, trouble and distance has changed. In the days before mass car ownership a daily round trip of up to twenty miles to school would have been hard-going.

The idea of enlarging Kinross Estate by lowering the level of Loch Leven was first proposed in the 1790s, but efforts to persuade other adjoining landowners and mill owners, who relied on the outfall from the loch as a source of power, took some time. The three-mile long New Cut, seen here, was begun in 1828 and four years later the loch's level had been reduced by four and a half feet, thus reclaiming a large amount of land. A look at the present-day map can still give some impression of how far the water receded because a number of roads and tracks can be seen heading for the loch, but stopping some way short of it. As well as being famous for its fish, the loch is also well-known for its bird, plant, insect and aquatic life. In order to protect this diversity Loch Leven was declared a National Nature Reserve in 1964 and all water sports other than angling were banned. Later that decade the Royal Society for the Protection of Birds (RSPB) bought Vane Farm at the south end of the loch. 'The Vane' used to be a favoured spot for gathering blaeberries, but the RSPB have now set up a reserve there with a splendid visitor centre and facilities for both dedicated ornithologists and curious amateurs to observe the bird life.

William Adam, architect and father of architects John and Robert Adam, purchased Blaircrambeth estate about 1733 and renamed it Blairadam. It was just north of the county's border with Fife, a man-made boundary that was not matched by the underlying geology. The northern edge of the West Fife Coalfield stretched past Kelty into Blairadam estate and provided work for miners who used to be one of Kinross-shire's most numerous groups of industrial workers. The railway running north from Cowdenbeath was therefore well placed to take out the coal worked on the estate, but Blairadam House had another connection with the North British Railway. William Patrick Adam, who became MP for Kinross and Clackmannan in 1859, was on its board of directors and his presence no doubt helped to guarantee the existence of Blairadam Station, seen here early in the twentieth century. It served a sparsely populated catchment area, a fact that was not lost on the London & North Eastern Railway which took over the NBR in 1923 and closed the station in 1930.

Cleish has impeccable religious associations. It was granted to Dunfermline Abbey in the twelfth or thirteenth century and was one of the early parishes that made up Kinross-shire. The village itself is small and peaceful, despite being at the centre of an ancient parish with a church that seems to have been up and down many times. It was regarded as an 'incommodious ruin' in 1775 when John Adam of Blairadam rebuilt it, and in 1832 a stove pipe became overheated setting fire to the wall plates, prompting another rebuilding. The tower and chancel were added in 1897. The manse too was rebuilt in 1744 and again in 1793, and given a new front in 1837. The tiny parochial school, across the road from the church, is noted for an adjacent schoolhouse that had box beds in the attic for boarders. Its schoolmaster in the late eighteenth century, William Michie, also had a claim to fame. He was a friend of Robert Burns who penned him an epitaph to be used when needed:

> Here lies Willie Michie's banes;
> O Satan! when ye tak him,
> Gie him the schulin o' your weans,
> For clever de'ils he'll mak them.

Loch Leven Castle's fame tends to overshadow the existence of the county's other fine castles, although the three shown here were houses rather than fortifications. Cleish Castle (top left) is a massive 70-foot high structure thought to date from the mid-sixteenth century, although it may span a period into the early seventeenth. It had fallen into disrepair by the mid-nineteenth century when it was restored and remodelled as a mansion house. Aldie Castle (top right), to the west of Cleish, consists of a four-storey tower, probably dating from the sixteenth century, with later additions enclosing an unusually small courtyard – about seven feet square. Aldie is thought to be named after Aldia Murray of Tullibardine who married into the Mercer family in the mid-fourteenth century and brought the lands with her. Tullibole Castle (lower right), near Crook of Devon, was built as a small mansion house in about 1608. It came into the Moncrieff family through marriage, and although the building was apparently unroofed for a time in the early nineteenth century, they later restored it to occupancy.

Blairingone is a quiet, unassuming village that people on the road between Kincardine and Kinross pass through and doubtless hardly notice – even if they do observe the speed limit! For busy city folk such a place might seem like a beacon of unchanging serenity in a world of constant flux, but Blairingone has indeed changed. Narrow footpaths and traffic calming have taken the place of the roadside trees and wide verges, and some of the buildings here have also gone. Nor has the village existed in a bubble of tranquillity. It was in the news in the 1860s when a baker's vanman from the village was robbed and murdered at Vicar's Bridge; his assailant, a poacher from Derbyshire, was hanged in Perth in one of Scotland's last public executions. More recently, a spate of nasty illnesses amongst villagers has been attributed to the disposal of effluent on nearby fields. But, just to ensure that Blairingone does not get uppity and assume its newsworthiness has propelled it onto the national stage, at least one major newspaper described it as being in Clackmannanshire!

The importance of mills to a rural economy is evident in place names like Milnathort and, as here, Powmill. At first glance this 1940s view of the A977 Kinross to Clackmannan road heading into Powmill from the east appears unaltered, but time has imposed some subtle changes. Apart from the loss of the prominent tree in the foreground, the road has been realigned to take a wider sweep and cross a new concrete bridge over the Gairney Burn, a tributary of the Devon. The bridge replaced an earlier stone one which can be seen in the centre of the picture – the lower section of the abutments are still there beside the new bridge. The field on the left is now the site of a roadside cafe and garden centre while the prominent hill in the background, Cult Hill, is in Fife; a reminder, if it were needed, of Kinross-shire's smallness. Pow is an old Scots word used to describe sluggish water and is the name given to the burn flowing through the flat land to the east of the village. A number of mills took their names from these pows, including another in Kinross-shire to the east of Loch Leven near Pittendreich.

This spectacular gorge was once one of Scotland's top scenic attractions, but with modern roads and fast cars able to take people further afield this forgotten gem has become a bypassed backwater. Here the River Devon crashes, roars and rumbles over rocks and cliff edges, squeezing through impossibly narrow defiles to find a way westward after its about-turn at Crook of Devon. The paths, fences and viewing platforms, so popular in Victorian days, were reinstated in 1984 by soldiers from the Royal Engineers. One of the attractions is the Devil's Mill, so-called because the movement of water through the rocks sounds like a mill turning – it never stops and, because only the devil works on the Sabbath, it must therefore be his mill! The double bridge is also a remarkable feature. The lower arch was made in 1713 by a William Grey of Saline. It is 86 feet above the rocky river and at only twelve feet wide, with no parapets, must have taken some nerve to cross. It was superseded in 1816 by the upper bridge which still carries traffic today.

With Rumbling Bridge offering the Victorian visitor a spectacular scenic attraction, the existence of a railway was likely to prove highly beneficial to the local tourist trade, but it took a while for a through route to be completed. The Devon Valley Railway was begun in the early 1850s with a short section from Alloa to Tillicoultry, and although the value of a continuation to Kinross was long recognised it was not authorised by Parliament until 1858. The track from Kinross to Rumbling Bridge had been laid by 1863, but work on the remainder of the line was not started until 1867. The section between Tilly and Dollar was opened in 1869 but the difficult Dollar to Rumbling Bridge link, which included the spectacular viaduct over the Gairney Burn, was not completed until 1871. It was a very scenic railway that would have been a boon to modern-day tourism, but passenger services were withdrawn in 1964. The section of line west of Dollar Mine stayed in operation for another ten years, but Rumbling Bridge Station was closed and the site has now been used for housing.

CROOK OF DEVON LOOKING WEST.

85316

The Devon is a river of many facets. From its source in the Ochil Hills it flows east and then tumbles south-east down Glendevon. On the flatter ground at the base of the hills it starts to flow east again, but at Crook of Devon it turns back on itself completely, a dramatic bend which gives the village its name. From here the river roars westward through the rocky gorge at Rumbling Bridge and meanders gently along the base of the Ochils to the Forth at Cambus. The river used to form the boundary between the counties of Kinross and Perth, but Crook of Devon was firmly in Kinross-shire. The village street here has changed little over the years although the omnipresent motor vehicle and traffic calming measures have superseded the lone carriage, and modern housing occupies the vacant area on the left. The tranquillity, however, masks Crook of Devon's dark past; in a field near here in 1662 a number of 'witches' were put to death by being strangled and then burned at the stake. It was done by nominally Christian people driven by fear and superstition who tried to explain events like a bad harvest or the death of a cow by claiming them to be the work of the Devil. Other people, usually women, were singled out to take the blame. They were tortured into confessing that they had links with Satan and had therefore played a part in the misfortune. It was not a good time to be different.

Carnbo straddles the A91 road between Milnathort and Stirling and is seen here looking west from where the present-day bus stops are sited. The road is wider now, with footpaths and kerbs which have made parking at the roadside, as a motorist has done here, a choice between ruining tyres or creating a hazard. The South Queich Burn spills off the Ochil Hills, goes under the road at the west end of Carnbo and runs to the south of the village and on to Tillyochie where it formerly drove a large woollen mill. The men of Carnbo and Tillyochie appear to have been good quoiters (pronounced kiters); in 1851 they beat a team from Auchterarder in a challenge match. The sport, in which a malleable iron ring was hurled about eighteen yards at a pin stuck in a bed of clay, is often associated with former mining communities, which makes its popularity in this rural place interesting. Quoiting greens were often sited next to pubs and the game was usually associated with gambling, although whether fortunes were won or lost in the game against Auchterarder is not known.

TILLYRIE. MILNATHORT.

People heading for the Ochil Hills Hospital passed through Tillyrie, a collection of houses and farms to the north of Milnathort. Their former owners used to be known as 'the brae lairds' presumably because of their location on rising ground. The large house of Nether Tillyrie enjoys superb views over Loch Leven and through the gap between Benarty and the Cleish Hills to the south. During the First World War it was used as a Voluntary Aid Detachment (VAD) Hospital for recuperating servicemen. The neighbouring hamlet of Upper Tillyrie is made up of a string of houses further up the hillside.

The Ochil Hills Hospital, to the north of Milnathort, was opened in 1901 as a private sanatorium for the treatment of tuberculosis. It was sited at an elevation of 1,000 feet above sea level to take advantage of the purer air at the higher altitude, and was set in 460 acres of grounds with sheltered walks in a pine wood. Sunshine was also regarded as a valuable treatment for those with pulmonary ailments and so the 60 bedrooms faced south, with magnificent views. The south-facing balcony in front of the foreground extension building would have been used to wheel bed-bound patients outside to take advantage of the sunshine. Being Scotland, of course, sunshine was not always available; nevertheless the patients would have been wheeled out to soak up the fresh air in all seasons and at all times of the day or night. The hospital was also advertised as having inhalation, electrical and hydropathic rooms, chemical and microscopical laboratories and a 'sun bath'. The building was later used as a convalescent home for hospitals in the Stirling area.

OCHIL HILLS HOSPITAL, MILNATHORT   B 7844

Reminiscence of an ancient Custom.
Blairhead Laird offering his thirlage at Burngrange ruined Mill, (Kinross.) Copyright D Gordon & Son, Cupar Fife

This early twentieth century postcard appears to portray the 'ancient custom' of thirlage as a subject for misty-eyed reminiscence, but this was one rural tradition that farming people were happy to see the back of. Peasant farmers were tied, or thirled, by their tenancies to take their grain to the laird's mill to have it ground, and to pay the laird a multure – usually a proportion of the ground meal – for the privilege. The farmers also had to help to keep the mill in good order by carrying out repairs and supplying it with new stones. Not surprisingly, all this made thirlage unpopular and attempts to evade it were commonplace. Also common was a general dislike of the miller and the mill; perhaps that is why this Burngrange Mill, beside the St Andrews road on the border with Fife, has been allowed to become a ruin – or maybe some farmers in the past indulged in another ancient custom and broke it – comprehensively!

The hamlet of Middleton, to the east of Tillyrie, has been somewhat overwhelmed by Middleton farm. Sheds and a silo now dominate the background of this view along an idyllic country lane between two cottages. The other dominant feature is the monkey puzzle tree in front of the cottage on the left. It is now so high that the building can be seen below the lower branches. In the mid-nineteenth century Middleton was noted for each house having at least one 70 year old occupant and the combined ages of the inhabitants being nearly 1,000 years. It must have been the hill air!

Anglers man the boats for a day of trout fishing on Loch Leven.

"A good catch of Lochleven Trout"

Loch Leven trout was famous for its unique pink flesh, and anglers came from all over the country hoping for a catch like this. By the 1990s, however, pollutants, which had built up over a long period of time, had caused the growth of blue-green algae in the water and this had drastically reduced the fish stocks, although steps have now been taken to help these recover. The loch was also famous in sporting circles for curling, as the stones nestling under the table behind the display of fish shows.